To Emily With Warm Wishes —
Gail Lamar

A Song for Lily

By Gail Lamar
Illustrations by Rhoda Pidgeon

For Emily
Best Wishes
Rhoda

Oxmoor House, Inc. Birmingham

Library of Congress Catalog Number: 82-80667
ISBN: 0-8487-0541-6

First Printing

A Song for Lily

Editor-in-Chief: John Logue
Editor: Karen Phillips Irons
Designer: Carol Middleton

To our husbands Lee and Guy
And to our children
Mary Jane, Catherine, Lee Jr., David, and Elizabeth

A Song for Lily

Through the deep, green woods
Ran a clear, cold creek
That prattled all the way to meet the sea.
On its dappled banks
Over thick and tangled ferns
Spread a great magnolia tree.

So broad its glossy leaves,
So close and dense they grew,
That only yellow wedges of the sun
Squeezed through,
To flitter for a moment,
Like butterflies in flight,
Till shadows crept about them
And snuffled out the light.

In a niche beneath the tree
Where the roots grew gnarled and mossy
And reached into the earth
To who-knows-where,
Lived seven darkeyed sisters,
Small as winter wrens,
With smooth and silky braids
Of crowblack hair.

They played all day
In the clear, cold creek,
That bright and breezy band,
Diving, dipping,
Eddyskipping,
Floating hand-in-hand.

But when darkness spread across the sky
And slipped between the trees,
The forest filled with twits and chittering,
Up and up the sisters climbed
In the great magnolia tree,
To lie on its broad leaves
To sing, to sing
Of ribboned rainbows
Blending, bending,
Lighting some enchanted place,
Of once upon a summertime
When sun and moon
Came face-to-face.

But there was one who only listened,
Her song was never heard—
Lily, who was youngest
And who could not speak a word.
Still her hopes were as bright
As her heart was light
And her smile as fresh and fair
As the tangle of tiny blossoms
That were braided through her hair.

She knew her sisters' music
And the music of the woods,
The ripple of an owl song from the pine,
The yapping of the vixen,
Skritching of the crickets
And the birring of the bees in the honeysuckle vine.

She cared for little creatures lost,
For birds with wounded wing
And always hoped, always wished
One day, some day to sing.

She wished on daisies, dandylions,
Wished on evening stars,
And though in silence every wish was sent,
They were heard within the hearts
Of all the beasts and birds
And they grieved for Lily and her mute lament.

They longed to help and combed the woods,
Searched them through and through
For medicines and magic herbs
And the place where the healall grew.

Rabbits searched the hedgerows,
Turtles searched the creek,
But not a single cure was found
And Lily could not speak.

Now an eagle who was passing by
And had seen the world with his eagle eye,
Knew each nook and hollow, cool and pied,
Knew crook and cave and cranny,
The burrows in the clover patch,
Knew every place on earth where hope might hide.

He told the strangest story
Of a woman called Hialeah:
"She lights the moon and scatters stars about,
Hurls the jagged thunderbolts
Across the stormy nights
And brings the rain to woodlands parched by drought.

"From the stream she made the river,
From the acorn sent the oak;
She tosses lathered waves upon the beach,
Guides the sun from east to west
And blows the clouds about.
Perhaps Hialeah can give young Lily speech.

"She camps," Eagle said, "where the asters bloom
At the foot of Deer Stand Hill
But summer goes and so must you
Before the winter's chill."

So it was the sisters went
To find the great Hialeah,
Early on a morning clean and bright,
Through the brush and trees and thickets,
Wending, winding up the pathways,
Spattered here and there with tattered light.
Spider spinnings strung the boughs,
Earthsounds filled the forest hush,
Fairyrings sprang everywhere
And towhees scratchdanced in the brush.

Their shadows ran before them
Through the thicket,
Before them flew the robin and the swallow.
By night the fireflies winked
Along the pathways
And little chorus frogs called "Follow! Follow!"

They traveled places strange and rare,
Through valleys cloaked in fog,
Up ridge and range where boulders met the sky;
Saw brooklets burnished by the sun,
Saw tumbling waterfalls
And passed the sleeping land of By-and-By.

The days slipped past
And into weeks
And time became so ravelled
That none could say
How far they'd come
Or just how long they'd traveled.

But the miles grew long
And the days grew short,
The nights grew dark as dread
And the sisters worried
As the greenwood slowly turned
From green to red.
Persimmon globes that once had hung
So fat and sweet and gold
Were tasteless now and bister-brown
And puckered by the cold.
Briars scratched their ankles,
Brambles caught their hair
And time and time the russet paths
Wound around to nowhere.

They longed for their tree
That never lost its leaves
At summer's end,
But on they wandered,
On and on,
Till down a hill and round a bend
There spread before the girls a meadow,
Deep in asters, blue as blue,
And Deer Stand Hill rose high behind it,
Autumn colors woven through.
Owl light had settled on the hill
But still there seemed to glow
A phosphorescent brightness
On hill and field below.
There came a voice as gentle
As ruffles through the wood,
That nearer, nearer drew
Until before the sisters stood
A splendid darkeyed woman
With long, black braided hair
And looking on her face they saw
Their own reflections there.

She knelt beside them in the grass,
Kissed each tiny head—
"Welcome, welcome, little ones!
I am Hialeah," she said.

She took them to a clearing
Where a campfire warmed the chill,
Gave them pears and chinquapins and tea,
Gave them wooly blankets,
Then Hialeah said,
"Tell me, daughters, why you've come to me."

"We've traveled many miles and moons
From the tree by the clear, cold creek.
We seek a song," they answered,
"For one who cannot speak."

They talked till the camp was lit by stars,
Was bathed by the white moonbeams,
Till seven heads began to nod
And soon were lost in dreams.
Dewdrops fell, the stars went out,
The moon slipped down the sky,
But deep in thought, Hialeah sat
And watched the embers die.

Early in the morning as the sun was peeping out,
She led them to a marsh
Where brown reeds grew.
One reed she cut and hollowed
And carved a tiny flute—
She put it to her lips and gently blew.
Winging notes flew everywhere
And lit upon the trees,
Tumbled through the bright November chill,
Tripped across the asters,
Hovered in the meadows
And sweet and clear they echoed from the hill.
Music of such beauty
That it touched the sisters' hearts,
Brought a tear to Lily, shy and mute.
Hialeah held her in her arms
And brushed the tear away,
Then tenderly she offered her the flute.

"Yours must be a wordless song,
But you shall have a song
To echo in the forest
Through every season long.

"You shall play
When summer rests upon the hillside,
When fall runs clean and sharp across the air,
When winter's frosty fingers hold the woodlands,
When spring comes softly like an answered prayer."

Though not a sound passed Lily's lips
The smile she smiled said more
Than a thousand tongues would ever tell
Or ever had before.
Her sisters smiled, the wind rejoiced
And sped the happy word
From highest hill to deepest vale
Till all the South had heard
That Lily had her dream, at last,
And though she still was mute,
The woods would soon be filled with sounds
Of Lily and her flute.

Hialeah taught her every note,
Every melody,
Then took them home to the waiting arms
Of the great magnolia tree.

Now at the end of a golden day
Lily climbs the tree and begins to play
Rhapsodies to the beasts and birds
And lullabies to the Milky Way.
When ice hangs from the sassafras,
When the creek becomes a looking glass,
When snowy blooms crown the great old tree
And winter's just a memory
The seven girls make music.
Still they play where the south wind blows,
Where the clear and prattledy cold creek flows,
Where the great, green, tall magnolia grows.

If you pass through a cool, deep wood
And the music rings so pure, so clear,
It's not the creek, not the loon,
Not the whip-o-will you hear
But seven tiny sisters near.

ABOUT THE AUTHOR

Gail Renfroe Lamar was born in Troy, Alabama, and attended the University of Alabama. An accomplished equestrienne, she conducted private lessons in horseback riding for several years. Then, with a grant from the Alabama Council for the Arts in conjunction with Auburn University, she represented the University Children's Theater throughout Alabama. Auburn, Alabama, is home for Gail, her husband and their three children.

ABOUT THE ARTIST

Rhoda Settle Pidgeon is a native of Berryville, Virginia. She studied art at Virginia Commonwealth University and has illustrated publications for the University of North Carolina and the University of Virginia. Rhoda lives with her husband and two children in Auburn, Alabama, where she works as medical illustrator for the Auburn University School of Veterinary Medicine.